Railways in Profile Series No. 3

GREAT WESTERN STATIONS

Compiled by G.Gamble

CHEONA PUBLICATIONS

© 1996 Cheona Publications

ISBN 1 900298 02 3

Production, design and setting by
Print-Rite, The Willows, School Lane,
Stadhampton, Oxford OX44 7TR

Printed by Alpha Print, Crawley, Oxon.

Published by
Cheona Publications
39 The Avenue, Chinnor, Oxfordshire OX9 4PD

PREFACE

A Great Western station was commonly recognisable from detail features of its construction and from its paintwork. Fittings were also characteristic and in the photographs which follow standard items such as water tanks, water cranes, platform trolleys and barrows, seats and fencing will be seen in many of the different locations. Variety in some of these instances is provided by stations of companies absorbed by the Great Western. Platform surfaces fell into five categories:- wooden planks, sandy grey paving stones 36" x 24" with similar but longer stones for the edging, (in some cases such edged platforms had medium grey asphalt or tarmac or even loose gravel instead of the paving stones). Some standard edged platforms had 10" x 5" blue paving bricks with a diamond patterned surface. The latter sometimes found use as edging when they had the rail-facing edge chamfered. Plain blue bricks were sometimes used for edging. Lastly there were plain bricks matching the normal paving slabs in colour.
Three main types of footbridge are found constructed of either steel or wood.
    (1) Simple type open to all the elements *(plate 20)*.
    (2) Similar style but fitted with a roof although the upper parts of the sides are still open *(plate 66)*.
    (3) A completely closed style *(plate 10)*.
Seats ranged from the early six-legged all wooden type *(see plate24)* to the first type with a cast iron end featuring a monogram of GWR *(see plate 74)* to the final cast end type with the 'shirt button' monogram. In BR days only the 'W' tended to be picked out in the painting *(see plate 102)*. At absorbed constituent stations e.g. Cambrian, that company's seats and sometimes Great Western ones could be seen together. A typical Cambrian platform seat is seen in *plate 118*.

Acknowledgements

All the photographs in this book are taken from the Nelson Collection by courtesy of Colin Judge to whom grateful thanks are extended also for the design and production work.
Thanks are also due to Ken Smith who has painstakingly produced the prints for this volume and whose photographic expertise over the last twenty years has enhanced the pictorial content and presentation of many important railway publications.

PHOTOGRAPHS

Copies of the photographs in this book, along with many other station subjects within the Nelson Collection, may be obtained via the publishers. No list of subjects is available at present but all enquiries, <u>with a stamped addressed envelope</u>, will be answered.

INTRODUCTION

This second volume in the **'Railways in Profile'** series portrays a variety of ex-Great Western Railway (or absorbed) stations and halts, chosen because of their potential as either subjects for modelling or to provide help for modellers seeking photographic details of aspects of station architecture, furniture, track layouts and all those features necessary to produce an accurate model.

Track plans of some of the stations have appeared in the excellent series *'An Historical Survey of Selected Great Western Stations - Layouts and Illustrations'* by R.H.Clark *(Volumes 1, 2 and 3)* and C.R Potts *(Volume 4):* published by Oxford Publishing Company between 1976 and 1985, but all long out of print. These are referred to where appropriate by 'GW1', 'GW2', 'GW3' or 'GW4' at the end of each caption with also the following abbreviations:

'T' : the date when the photograph was taken.

'P' : the date when the station/halt closed to passenger traffic.

'F' : the date when the station/halt closed to freight services, where relevant or possible.

N.B. 'F'. The date given here does not take into account goods traffic to private sidings which may have continued after the station closed for ordinary freight workings.

PAINTING

For many years 'light' stone and 'dark' stone were the basic colours used. These varied because they were normally mixed on site, to match a colour card, by adding the 'required' amount of iron oxide to a white lead base. Chocolate was used in instances and from the early 1930's a maroon-brown was used for situations subject to hard wear. From 1946 an all-cream scheme was introduced for all exterior situations except nameplates, nameboards and parts of signalboxes. Because of the war this style did not spread far over the system and when Nationalisation came in 1948, the Western Region of British Railways standardised on a chocolate and cream colour scheme for woodwork, and interiors were often painted dark battleship grey. These colours did not penetrate the full system and there were instances where stations closed in the 1960's or after the Beeching report but were still in weathered light and dark stone.

Most of the following photographs were taken between 1951 and 1964 and consequently a variety of colour schemes can be seen.

For details on Great Western colour schemes the reader is referred to *'Great Western Way'* by J.N.Slinn, published by the Historical Model Railway Society (at present out of print) ISBN 0 902 835033.

BIBLIOGRAPHY

1. An Historical Survey of Selected Great Western Stations - Layouts and Illustrations - Volume 1
    by R.H.Clark *published by* Oxford Publishing Company. 1976   0 902 88829 3
2.   *As above but* Volume 2. 1979   0 860 93015 7
3.   *As above but* Volume 3. 1981   0 860 93111 0
4.   *As above but* Volume 4 by C.R.Potts. 1985   0 860 93191 1
5. GWR Branch Lines *by* C.J.Gammell *published by* Oxford Publishing Co. 1995   0 860 93521 3
6. Great Western Way *by* J.N.Slinn *published by* Historical Model Rly. Soc. 1985   0 902 83503 3
7. British Railways Pre-Grouping Atlas & Gazetteer *published by* Ian Allan Ltd 1972   0 711 00320 3
8. Passengers No More (2nd edition) *by* G.Daniels & L.Dench
    published by Ian Allan Ltd. 1964   0 711 00438 2
9. Clinker's Register of Closed Passenger Stations and Goods Depots in England, Scotland and Wales
    1830 - 1980 *by* C.R.Clinker *published by* Avon Anglia Publications and Services 1988 0 905 46691 8
10. A Pictorial Record of Great Western Architecture
    by A. Vaughan *published by* Oxford Publishing Company. 1977   0 902 88822 6

Plate 1. **PENHELIG HALT**. Situated on the Cambrian Coast line one mile east of Aberdovey, this view looking towards Penhelig tunnel and Dovey Junction. Access was via the steps between the nameboard and the shelter/office. The side windows in the office enabled staff to see approaching up trains. Note the two rails by the board crossing to accommodate a permanent way maintenance trolley. (T.9/7/1964).

Plate 2. **PENHELIG HALT**. This time looking towards Aberdovey with Craig-y-Don tunnel in view. Note generally the Scots pines, bridges at both ends of the planked extensions to the platforms and the lamp brackets. The 1960 timetable shows that the Pwllheli portion of the Cambrian Coast Express called here. (T.9/7/1964).

Plate 3. **MALMESBURY**. Looking towards the buffer stops at the end of the branch from Little Somerford. The canopy is angled to clear coaches and the stone station building blends in with the local buildings. Note the white paling fence and the hand winch for use in unloading at the end loading dock, to the left. (T.21/5/1958; P.10/9/1951; F.12/11/1962)

Plate 4. **MALMESBURY**. Viewed towards Little Somerford with the Abbey ruins in the background. Note the ornate canopy supports, large stone goods shed and single road wood and stone engine shed (all that remains today) - a sub shed of Swindon 82C. (T.21/5/1958)

Plate 5. **WESTON-SUPER-MARE**. Viewed in the up direction. Designed by Francis Fox and erected in 1882, the stone buildings have superb ornate canopies. Note the large glazed bridge, two water tanks and the staff dealing with one of those important 'internal user' boxes. The local Odeon cinema was showing the film about the 'Triffids'. (T. 6/5/1953; F. 20/6/1966)

Plate 6. **WESTON-SUPER-MARE**. From the same spot as above but looking in the down direction. Note the intricate supports for the canopy, the wealth of advertising boards, platform trolleys, enamel station signs and the more recent illuminated station name indicators. The signalbox was accessed from the ramp at the end of the sharply curving platform. (T.6/5/1953)

Plate 7. **LLANGOLLEN**. Looking towards Ruabon showing the typical footbridge, the signalbox on the platform, adjacent signals, water column and loading gauge. The touring coaches have crossed the River Dee bridge on their way into town. (GW4; T.10/8/1961; P. 18/1/1965; F. 1/4/1968)

Plate 8. **LLANGOLLEN**. Viewed towards Corwen with the River Dee rushing relentlessly around the rocks. The long curving platforms (due to the course of the river) have small waiting rooms towards the western ends with 'Gentlemen's' accommodation in the one on the right. Note the water tank and the high terraced houses which still overlook an active railway, now operated by the Llangollen Railway (from 13/9/1975) (T. 10/8/1961)

Plate 9. **KIDDERMINSTER**. Looking towards Worcester with an ex-GWR pannier tank shunting the cavernous goods shed (now used by the Severn Valley Railway). Note the exterior framed, glazed footbridge with smoke deflectors and how the signalbox steps come down to their own extension of the platform. (T. 25/5/1961; F. 4/1983

Plate 10. **KIDDERMINSTER**. Looking towards Birmingham with a clear view of the footbridge roof and the extension to the left hand platform under the Bromsgrove road bridge. Note the coal in the foreground, dislodged from the tender of a locomotive when using the water crane. The proximity of the buffer stop to the signalbox leaves little margin for error when shunting! (T. 25/5/1961)

Plate 11. **CHIPPING NORTON**. From the A44 road bridge looking towards Kingham and showing the simple lattice footbridge with its two lamps and the stone station buildings with large goods shed and office. Note the different platform surfaces and the ornate valances to the platform canopies.
(GW1; T. 20/8/1956; P. 3/12/1962; F. 7/9/1964)

Plate 12. **CHIPPING NORTON**. Looking towards Hook Norton from the end of the down platform. Note the paling fence to the barrow crossing, complex trackwork, signal wires and point rodding, the water tower and station building. The small upside waiting room shelter has its roof extended to form a canopy.
(T. 20/8/1956)

Plate 13. **HEMYOCK**. A close up view of the wooden ground frame hut (Hemyock East Ground Frame) and the Arthur Pain design station buildings, looking towards the end of the line. Note the end details of the station buildings, fire buckets (red with black lettering), the old platform lamp post and rail supports for the station nameboard. All spoiled by that oil drum! (GW1; T. 5/1951; P. 9/9/1963; F. 6/9/1965)

Plate 14. **HEMYOCK**. Looking at the station from near the gated entrance to the dairy sidings. Note the cattle dock with adjacent catch point, white paling fence on the platform and the incongruous breeze block extension to the station building. The water tower, yard crane and store are just visible in the distance. (T. 5/1951)

Plate 15. **HEMYOCK**. Viewed from near the water tower showing the up end of the station buildings and the dairy in the background. At this time the dairy was served by the siding seen on the right and the one running behind the station building which went through the goods shed! (T. 5/1951)

Plate 16. **HEMYOCK**. The rear of the station building with its pipes and vents and the dairy building beyond. Note the sliding door on the station building allowing for on-and off loading of parcels from road vehicles. (T. 5/1951)

Plate 17. **CHURSTON**. Seen from the double arched Brixham road bridge north of the station. The Brixham branch train waits in the bay platform. Note the two signals giving access to the branch and the up starter on the right. A mass of point rodding originates from the signalbox just beyond the stone station building on the down platform. The cattle dock siding is protected by a catch point. (GW3; T.5/1951); P.1972*; F.4/12/1967) * Re-opened by Torbay Steam Railway in 1973.

Plate 18. **CHURSTON**. Looking in the up direction from the bay platform. Note the Brixham branch shelter, platform trolley, asbestos(!) roofing, gas lamps and water tower. The cast sign on the left is mounted on a length of old bridge rail. The stone road bridge with its two unequal arches is carrying a veteran car - note how the branch and main line rapidly diverge beyond the bridge. (T. 5/1951)

Plate 19. **BRIDGNORTH**. Looking north from the footbridge. The scene is very similar today except for the Severn Valley Railway locomotive sheds on the left. The stone station building with its ornate gable ends, signalbox and waiting shelter are unchanged. Note the boarded walkway over the point rodding and the different platform surfaces, left and right. (T. 25/5/1961: P. 9/9/1963*; F. 2/12/1963) * Re-opened by the Severn Valley Railway in 1970.

Plate 20. **BRIDGNORTH**. Looking south from by the signalbox showing the fine lattice footbridge with numerous permanent way department buildings beyond. Platform barrows and trolleys await business! The line climbs and curves going south. (T. 25/5/1961)

Plate 21. **MONMOUTH (TROY)**. With the line to Ross straight ahead and the Wye Valley route to Chepstow rising and curving right to go over the viaduct. The fine station building on the left has an elaborate canopy whilst that on the right is an extension of the roof. The station staff take the sun whilst awaiting the arrival of the next train.(T. 6/5/1948; P. 5/1/1959; F. 6/1/1964)

Plate 22. **NEWBRIDGE ON WYE**. Looking north towards Llanidloes. A small neat Cambrian-built station building with prominent bay windows all spoiled by the later brick extension. The stone-faced platforms are slightly staggered and the wooden signalbox and goods shed stand next to one another. The signs to the right of the signal warn 'Passengers about crossing the line...' with 'Beware of Trains' (on the top). (T. 1/6/1961; P. 31/12/1962; F. 31/12/1962)

Plate 23. **BEWDLEY**. Looking south along the bricked surface where the platform was extended. The scene is much the same today with the open roofed footbridge leading to island platforms 2 and 3, the latter being used for the Tenbury Wells and Wooferton branch services. The goods yard is hidden by the station building but part of the goods shed can just be seen. Bewdley South Box is just visible in the distance. (T. 25/5/1961; P. 5/1/1970*; F. 1/2/1965) * Re-opened by the Severn Valley Railway 18/5/1974.

Plate 24. **BEWDLEY**. This time looking north towards Bridgnorth from platform 1 showing the station building (no canopy) and Bewdley North Box just beyond the underslung starting signals - normal height signals would have been obscured by the footbridge. Beyond the signalbox is the stone parapet of Bewdley viaduct. (T. 25/5/1961)

Plate 25. **BRENT**. Looking towards Plymouth with a busy scene on the Kingsbridge bound platform where an ex-GWR 2-6-2T is in charge of a mixed train and a freight stands on the next line. Note the signalbox on the platform, the large goods shed and office and the cattle dock on the left. The instruction on the station nameboard is for the benefit of the Kingsbridge branch passengers. A classic scene only marred by the telegraph poles and wires, however the foreground boundary fence is quite new. (GW2; T. 12/5/1951; P. 5/10/1964; F. 6/4/1964)

Plate 26. **BRENT**, from the road *bridge (seen in plate 25)*. Note the complex pointwork and the permanent way spares. The plants grown on the platform here always gave an air of the Mediterranean to the station. (T. 12/5/1951)

Plate 27. **MUCH WENLOCK**, on the line from Buildwas to Craven Arms, looking towards the latter, showing the large brick and stone station building with ornate fleur de lys embellishments to the roof ridge and the well kept gardens and flower beds. Note the unusual water column, large signalbox and the profusion of conifers. (T. 18/5/1961; P. 23/7/1962; F. 2/12/1963)

Plate 28. **MUCH WENLOCK** from near to the signalbox looking towards Buildwas. Note the station nameboard (white letters on a black background) with concrete supports, fire buckets, covered platform trolley, corrugated iron hut with its mandatory bicycle and the ornate station lamp. (T. 18/5/1961)

Plate 29. **DULVERTON**. Looking towards Taunton. Notice the gas supply pipes on the end of the station canopy and the small plate 'Danger Live Wires' nearby! The notice hanging from the footbridge reads 'TO EXE VALLEY TRAINS'. The waiting room on the right is built of stone edged with light coloured bricks and has a slate roof. Note the old style wooden platform seat (right) with one of those useless wire waste baskets nearby and the yard crane just visible to the left of the waiting room. (GW1; T. 9/5/1951; P. 3/10/1966; F. 6/7/1964)

Plate 30. **DULVERTON**. Showing the random stone goods shed, a gas-type platform lamp and the fine lattice footbridge. Note the platform-sited starter signal for the westbound loop line trains and also the cattle pens to the left. (T. 9/5/1951)

Plate 31. **AXBRIDGE**. Looking towards Wells. The signalbox was resited in 1907, and in 1924 the large goods shed and covered loading area were added. Note the exquisite Bristol & Exeter Railway style bargeboards, the station lamps with winders to lower the brackets and the various renovations to the platform edges. (GW1; T. 17/9/1958; P. 9/9/1963; F. 10/6/1963)

Plate 32. **AXBRIDGE**, this time looking towards Yatton and showing the simple wooden shelter with ornate bargeboards, the fine rock garden and the old GWR platform seat - all contrasting with the rather austere plate footbridge. (T. 17/9/1958)

Plate 33. **WELLS (TUCKER STREET).** Looking towards Shepton Mallet with ex-LMS Ivatt 2-6-0 No. 46525 - a local engine, about to shunt the branch freight. The stone station buildings show similar Bristol & Exeter Railway features to those at Axbridge. The signalbox is just visible at the end of the up platform - the box beyond the watercrane is on the Somerset & Dorset line. (The two lines joined beyond the factory buildings on the left). The right-hand siding originally had a turntable. (GW1; T. 19/9/1958; P. 9/9/1963; F. 13/7/1964)

Plate 34. **WELLS (TUCKER STREET).** Viewed towards Yatton showing the superb stone roadbridge. Note the well kept gardens and water crane with its fire devil. The goods yard is beyond the bridge on the right. (T. 19/9/1958)

Plate 35. **FARINGDON**. The locomotive shed, (a sub shed to 82C Swindon), just over two years after closure. A single road slate-roofed Cotswold stone building, with office at the side and sleeper-built stockade store. Note the large ecclesiastical style windows. (GW1; T. 19/5/1953; P. 31/12/1951; F. 1/7/1963)

Plate 36. **FARINGDON**. From the buffer stops looking towards Uffington. The stone station building has a combined roof and canopy with large wooden brackets. Freight only operated by this time, the platform end ground frame has gone and the lighter patches on the station wall show where noticeboards were placed. (T. 19/5/1958)

Plate 37. **FARINGDON**. Looking towards the buffer stops with the loading dock (centre) and cattle pens just beyond. The large goods shed and yard crane are still in use. Note the odd shape to the roof of the station building with its centrally placed chimneys. (T. 19/5/1958)

Plate 38. **SHIPSTON-ON-STOUR**. From the platform end looking towards Moreton-in-Marsh, when the station was still in use for freight traffic. Note the ex-GWR Iron Mink 'For use at Shipston-on-Stour',(No.064358), cattle pens, loading gauge, permanent way hut and locomotive shed to the left. (GW1; T. 20/8/1956; P. 8/7/1929; F. 2/5/1960)

Plate 39. **SHIPSTON-ON-STOUR**. With the branch freight in the platform road. The large austere goods shed contrasts with the old passenger brake van mounted on stilts. (T. 20/8/1956)

Plate 40. **SHIPSTON-ON-STOUR**. From the buffer stops with the loading dock on the left. The station building is unusual being of exterior panelled timber construction with a half-platform width canopy fitted with a deep valance. Weeds are beginning to grow on the platform and nature is taking over the flower beds. (T. 20/8/1956)

Plate 41. **KEMBLE**. Looking towards Gloucester as an up train arrives headed by ex-GWR 2-6-2T No. 6137 piloting a Hymek diesel. The canopies with their deep, ornate end valances give way to an unusual footbridge. The central part over the tracks is typical open style with roof but on the right, the lattice work is boarded in and at the two ends the bridge is fully glazed. The signalbox can be seen at the end of the down platform, to the left of which was the Tetbury branch bay platform. (GW1; T. 10/5/1963;F. 1/8/1967)

Plate 42. **KEMBLE**. Again looking towards Gloucester but showing the Cirencester branch platform with its extensive canopy and an AC Cars 4-wheeled railbus has the signal for its journey down the branch. Note the position of the arm of the up main starter (not obscured by the footbridge). An arboreous station with a curious water tank beyond the signalbox. (East signalbox was closed in 1929 - being sited on the down platform opposite the end of the up platform). (T. 10/5/1963)

Plate 43. **CHEPSTOW**. Looking west towards Newport with the pleasant Brunelian 'chalet' style stone building, with its bay window and almost horizontal canopy, on the down island platform - contrasting with the angled one on the waiting shelter on the up platform. The smart flower beds, the horse chestnut trees and the neatly arranged platform seats all seem a generation away from the modern platform lamps. (T. 1/6/1964; F. 7/4/1969)

Plate 44. **CHEPSTOW**. Viewed in the same direction as plate 43 but showing the roofed, rivetted, open style footbridge with the typical GWR signalbox beyond and also the goods shed. Plenty of interesting trackwork, signals, a water crane and a large water tank. (T. 1/6/1964)

Plate 45. **CHEPSTOW**. Looking east towards Lydney and supplying a fine view of the footbridge and the up platform building - similar to the down one but with the added waiting shelter. The small kiosk is for the ticket collector and note the station nameboard with the lower part obliterated, (this part referred to the Wye Valley line trains which ran into the left hand side of the island platform. This line closed to passengers on the 5th January, 1959). (T. 1/6/1964)

Plate 46. **CHEPSTOW**. From the eastern end of the up platform showing the elevated curve of the line to cross the famous bridge over the River Wye (just visible). The underslung girder span being a replacement for Brunel's earlier masterpiece. Notice how narrow the extensions to the platforms are here and the '3 car/6 car' signs to give drivers a guide as to where to stop. (T. 1/6/1964)

Plate 47. **STOURBRIDGE TOWN**. The original station seen from the footbridge but with platform and track cut back to the station side of the bridge over Foster street. The station building is an example of the GWR standard 'turreted' design. Note the grounded van body and the brown and cream enamel sign. The independent line on the right leads on to Stourbridge Goods and Wharf terminus. (GW4;T.12/10/1961;F.7/1965 [Stourbridge Goods])

Plate 48. **STOURBRIDGE WHARF and GAS WORKS**. With the huge goods shed/warehouse and its canal side loading bay on the right. To the left ex-GWR 0-6-0 pannier tank No.9724 (devoid of both smokebox and cabside number plates) deals with wagons being loaded with gravel. Note the superb yard lamp and its 'lean to's'; the wharf crane and the wagon sheet near the locomotive. (T. 15/7/1965)

Plate 49. **STOURBRIDGE (GOODS)**. With Stourbridge Town behind the photographer, the overgrown siding seen on the right, served the canal. Note the huge two-road goods shed, the conical water tower and the lone yard lamp. All this was eradicated in 1965. (T. 12/10/1961; F. 5/7/1965)

Plate 50. **CULHAM**. Looking towards Oxford from the up platform, showing the fine lattice footbridge with Brunelian 'roadside' station buildings and goods shed beyond. The signalbox can just be seen opposite the goods shed whilst the brick wall on the left belongs to the Railway Hotel. Repair work is underway on the down platform. (GW1; T. 18/6/1964; F. 19/7/1965)

Plate 51. **CULHAM**. Seen from the station approach road on the upside. The station building was erected 3 or 4 years after the similar one at Pangbourne and clearly shows the all-round awning with no valance. Note the cast iron brackets supporting the awning, the steep pitch of the roof and the diamond-shaped chimney. The signalbox is on the extreme right. (T. 18/6/1964)

Plate 52. **FROME**. Viewed towards Westbury, showing the fine overall roof - the last GWR train shed in regular use (designed by J.R.Hannaford - one of Brunel's assistants). The station lamps are more recent as is the enamel nameboard. Note the fire bucket stand and the additional station canopy beyond the footbridge. (GW3; T. 11/5/1963)

Plate 53. **WELSHPOOL**. Looking towards Shrewsbury showing the covered, rivetted, plate footbridge, the island platform buildings beyond and the splendid brick water tower with adjacent yard crane. Note the ornate lamp and the relatively narrow platforms. (GW3; T. 3/8/1961)

Plate 54. **WELSHPOOL**. The very long station building with its unique awning is seen from the road bridge at the Newtown end of the station. The station nameboard relates to its pre-1965 importance. (T. 3/8/1961)

Plate 55. **WELSHPOOL**. Looking west. The point rodding runs from the signalbox at the eastern end of platform 3. Note the steel ties between adjacent sleepers on the 'up' main. The ornate brackets supporting the awning show up well as does the asymmetrical arrangement of the platform limbs of the footbridge. (T. 3/8/1961)

Plate 56. **BRYMBO**. Viewed towards Croes Newydd. A basic station with a wooden boarded building and a corrugated iron store. Fine spear-headed fencing protects the walkway to the near platform which has a GWR style pagoda shelter. A simple open footbridge once spanned the tracks from the near end of the station building. This station was not too accessible for the population who lived at a higher level and many of them used the more convenient Brymbo West Halt. (T. 15/5/1948; P. 27/3/1950; F. 2/11/1964)

Plate 57. **BRYMBO**. With the steelworks in the distance and a splendid array of signals - the long fixed distant arm (left) and the backing signals (with 2 holes in the arms), all controlled by Brymbo Middle Signalbox (right) as well as the adjacent level crossing gates. Note the short steelworks admission signal arm below the long fixed distant. Other details include the water tank, milepost and the fine GWR trespass notice with a 'forty shillings fine or one month imprisonment in default'! (T. 15/5/1948)

Plate 58. **CLEOBURY MORTIMER**. Looking west towards Tenbury Wells. The austere waiting shelter for Bewdley-bound passengers contrasts with the grand station buildings, typical of those in the Severn Valley area. To the right of the signalbox and behind the wire and post fence was Cleobury Mortimer and Ditton Priors Light Railway territory. Note the three watertanks. (T. 6/7/1961; P. 1/8/1962; F. 6/1/1964)

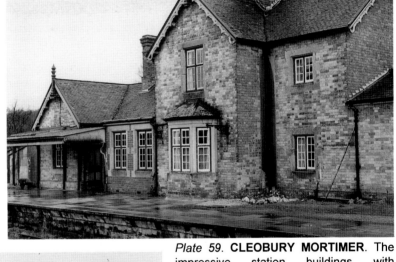

Plate 59. **CLEOBURY MORTIMER**. The impressive station buildings with decorative bargeboards - except for one on the left! There is a fine lamp bracket by the bay window and a 'You may telephone from here' sign. Note the stone surrounds to the windows. (T. 6/7/1961)

Plate 60. **CLEOBURY MORTIMER**. With an ex-GWR pannier tank shunting in the Admiralty sidings (ex CM & DPLR). The track is getting overgrown but there is plenty of signal and water tank detail and even a drunken telegraph pole! (T. 6/7/1961)

Plate 61. **BIRMINGHAM (MOOR STREET)**. From platform 2 with its massive steel and glass canopy contrasting with the smaller version on the right hand platform. Note the 'open' and 'closed' platform seats and the traverser by the buffer stops to release train locomotives. The background buildings would be a challenge to any would be modeller! (GW4; T. 5/10/1961; F. 6/11/1972)

Plate 62. **BIRMINGHAM (MOOR STREET)**. Looking towards Tyseley with the huge two road goods shed on the right, a large water tower and a fine collection of signals (including the down starter to Snow Hill (left) which has a colour light distant below the semaphore). Moor Street signalbox controlled the station and the through lines to Snow Hill. (T. 5/10/1961)

Plate 63. **CHEDDAR**. The exterior of this splendid station building, made from crafted local stone, exudes the architectural affluence of the Bristol & Exeter Railway. From the finely decorated ridges, patterned tiles to the ornate gable ends and superb chimneys with terra-cotta pots.
(GW1; T. 19/9/1958; P. 9/9/1963; F. 29/11/1965)

Plate 64. **CHEDDAR**. Looking towards Wells from inside the fine overall roof - the excessive width between the platforms is a relic of broad gauge days. Note the old pattern seat and the large amount of parcel traffic. (T. 19/9/1958)

Plate 65. **CHEDDAR**. The superb massive stone goods shed and the Saxby & Farmer signalbox at the Yatton end of the station.
(T. 19/9/1958)

Plate 66. **BOX**. The splendid roofed lattice footbridge, looking towards Bath with the water tank, permanent way hut and offices and the siding-to-down-main starting signal, all visible in the distance. (GW2; T. 6/5/1963; P. 4/1/1965; F. 10/6/1963)

Plate 67. **BOX**. A superb view of the station and tunnel mouth taken from the road bridge on the Bath side of the station. Note the intricate trackwork, the various buildings on the left including the water tower, two yard cranes and the tall down main start and repeater signal (necessary because of the curved approach to the station from the tunnel). An engine shed (closed 1919) stood between the permanent way buildings and the water tower. (T. 6/5/1963)

Plate 68. **HIGHBRIDGE**. Looking towards Bristol with the wooden GWR Highbridge West signalbox (the other end was wedged-shaped) and the open concrete footbridge. The diagonal crossing line is the Somerset and Dorset Railway to Burnham-on-Sea. Beyond is the large single road goods shed. Note the centre balance signals, the number of platform trolleys and the complex trackwork. (T. 6/5/1963; F. 2/11/1964)

Plate 69. **HIGHBRIDGE**. Looking towards Bridgwater. Platforms 6 &7 are GWR whereas 1 to 5 were Somerset & Dorset Railway - all lying behind the station building on platform 6. The concrete footbridge was not GWR inspired. (T. 6/5/1963)

Plate 70. **MONTGOMERY**. Looking towards Welshpool. The signalbox has an unusual corrugated roof and there is a tablet post next to the steps as this was a passing place on the Cambrian Welshpool to Moat Lane Junction line. A re-roofing operation is taking place on the station building - note the steep pitch of the various gables and the very tall chimneys. (T. 27/7/1961; P. 14/6/1965; F. 4/5/1964)

Plate 71 **MONTGOMERY**. A fine view of the station building - roof work completed! An abundance of windows including a large one on the bay and a huge one in the booking hall with a Cambrian seat in front of it. Note the square signal post and as well as being able to post a letter, one could also 'telephone from here'. (T. 10/10/1963)

Plate 72. **MONTGOMERY**. Note the small wooden waiting shelter for passengers to Newtown, the smart platform lamps, large goods shed and signalbox. Repair work on the station roof hasn't enhanced its appearance. (T. 27/7/1961)

Plate 73. **MALVERN LINK**. Looking towards Worcester. Sumptuous random stone ecclesiastical style buildings with extensive decorative canopies. The concrete platform lamps are incongruous late intrusions. Note the variety of advertisement boards and the sighting 'patch' painted on the bridge for the starting signal (T. 3/5/1962; F. 1/6/1964)

Plate 74. **THEALE**. Looking towards Newbury. The red brick, with window and door arches picked out in yellow is characteristic of the Brunelian 'chalet' style station buildings on the Berks and Hants line as is the all-round canopy. The rivetted plate footbridge has a corrugated roof - note the ornate station lamps and the GWR platform seats. (T. 9/5/1963; F. 1/7/1970)

Plate 75. **THEALE**. Showing the small wooden waiting shelter on the down platform and the signalbox with the large wooden broad gauge type goods shed beyond. Note how the end wall on the main building has had to be shored up. (T. 9/5/1963)

Plate 76. **UFFCULME**. Looking towards Hemyock with the diminutive station building on the left and the small shed/store beyond. The poster boards have been well used. Note the small station sign and the 'Season tickets must be shown here' - both white lettering on blue enamel background. The platform surface is of variable construction and leads on to the raised footway across the bridge over the river Culm. The post and rail fence on the right seems to be falling into the river!
(GW1; T. 5/5/1951; P. 9/9/1963; F. 8/5/1967)

Plate 77. **UFFCULME**. With the cattle pens on the left (behind the sheeted wagons) and the small level crossing surrounded by white paling fences. The massive buildings of G.Small and Sons (Devon) Ltd - Agricultural Merchants - dominate the scene. (T. 5/5/1951)

Plate78. **BISHOP'S LYDEARD**. Looking towards Taunton. The neat station building with its restricted canopy and the wood and stone goods shed are Bristol & Exeter Railway designs. The up platform only has a small wooden waiting shelter and a corrugated iron store. (GW1; T. 11/9/1957; P. 4/1/1971*; F. 6/7/1964) * Re-opened by the West Somerset Railway in June 1979.

Plate 79. **LOOE**. From a common location but unobscured by a train. The small water tank is reminiscent of a narrow gauge facility. Few platform lamps but plenty of seats, barrows and trolleys. The poster above the fire buckets is advertising 'Each Monday to Friday to Plymouth and return 4/3d' (approximately 22p!). Note the platelayer's hut just before the starter signal for Liskeard. (GW2; T. 9/5/1956; F. 4/11/1963)

Plate 80. **ASHBURTON**. The terminus of the branch from Totnes, viewed from across the approach road and showing the fine overall roof with the attached stone station building. Note the industrial buildings on the right and the veteran cars, plus the 'veteran'! (T. 14/9/1959; P. 3/11/1958; F. 10/9/1962)

Plate 81. **ASHBURTON**. Viewed from the single line in from Totnes with the stone locomotive shed on the right and the fine backdrop of Ashburton village behind the station. The large goods shed can be seen in the distance, just above the goods van. (T.14/9/1959)

Plate 82. **HIGHWORTH**. With sidings on the left and the main running line to Swindon curving away on a lower level to the right. The wooden goods shed has a steeply pitched roof and there is a large gap above the door! Plenty to note here - the wooden-posted starter signal with a wooden arm, the superb platform lamp, the spear-headed fencing and the engineering brick surface to the platform. Point and signal controls come from Highworth Ground Frame (8 levers, 1 and 8 spare). The point disc on the right was self activating (not lever controlled like a normal ground signal). (GW1; T. 23/8/1956; P. 2/3/1953*; F. 6/9/1962) * Workmen's trains to Swindon Works ran until 6/8/1962.

Plate 83. **HIGHWORTH**. Showing the basic wooden station building and the ground frame hut. We see here how the track curves beyond the station passing the loading bank and sheep pens to the buffer stops, just hidden by the corrugated iron hut. The large station house is seen on the right. All long gone! (T. 23/8/1956)

Plate 84. **STONEHOUSE**. Looking towards Stroud and showing the fine Brunelian stone buildings, including one Brunel chimney (left - the others are replacements) and full wooden canopies with decorative iron supporting brackets. The huge goods shed and yard crane can be seen beyond the signalbox and the open topped plate footbridge. Note the dip in the right hand platform, only rectified in 1976 during re-building. (T. 3/5/1962; F. 28/12/1964)

Plate 85. **STONEHOUSE**. Looking towards Gloucester showing the crossover in the station and the classic stone waiting room with an all round canopy. Note the change in the platform facing material indicating an extension at some time. (T. 3/5/1962)

Plate 86. **DEVYNOCK and SENNYBRIDGE**. On the former Neath and Brecon line, looking towards Brecon. The N & B stone station building has had a replacement chimney - note how little ballast there is on the nearside track. (GW2; T. 1/5/1962; P. 15/10/1962; F. 15/10/1962)

Plate 87. **DEVYNOCK and SENNYBRIDGE**. Looking towards Neath and showing the different materials used for the platform surface. The large wooden planked goods shed and the signalbox are also N & B design. Situated 24½ miles from Neath. (T. 1/5/1962)

Plate 88. **AYNHO**. Photographed looking north towards Aynho Junction - the flyover carries the down mainline from Princes Risborough. Two fine stone buildings but with disappointing canopies except for the lion's masks. The signalbox controlled what is seen here - beyond the flyover is Aynho Junction box. Note the fire buckets and the neat flower beds contrasting with the untidy platform surfaces and the unsightly tanks mounted on the waiting room. (T. 28/5/1964; P. 2/11/1964; F. 4/5/1964)

Plate 89. **AYNHO (FOR DEDDINGTON)** - the latter being a larger settlement than Aynho and about 2 miles east of the station. This is the view looking almost south from the disused goods yard with some fine spear-headed fencing and the typical GWR signalbox on the up platform. (T. 28/5/1964)

Plate 90. **DURSTON**. With the line to Bridgwater going straight ahead whilst the line curving to the right goes to Athelney and Langport. The signalbox is unusual - at 90º to the running lines. Note how the two platform buildings differ in roof, canopy and general design. The advertisements (right) refer to excursions to Yeovil and Taunton, Bertram Mills Circus and Holidays in Ireland. (T. 1/9/1957; P. 5/10/1964; F. 6/7/1964)

*Plate 91.***DURSTON**. Looking towards Cogload Junction from the footbridge. New ballast has been laid and workmen are operating beyond the roadbridge. Ex-GWR 0-6-0 pannier tank No. 5771 indulges in a spot of shunting - note the water column with its fire devil, 'Passenger.... to cross' signs, starting signals and a very short headshunt! (T. 1/9/1957)

Plate 92. **CLEVEDON**. Terminus of the short branch from Yatton. Note the overall roof, the double canopy with ornate supports and valancing and the superb broad gauge period water tank - now regrettably all gone! Who left his case behind? (GW1; T. 17/9/1958; P. 3/10/1966; F. 10/6/1963)

Plate 93. **CLEVEDON**. Looking towards Yatton. The austere signalbox contrasts with the sumptuous Bristol & Exeter Railway stone goods shed (with its ornate doorway) - a fine subject for a model. (T. 17/9/1958)

Plate 94. **RADSTOCK**. Situated on the Bristol to Frome line, looking here towards Frome with the simple wooden waiting shelter (left) and the robust stone station building (right). The goods shed and yard are to the right behind the small, neat water tank. (T. 17/9/1958; P. 2/11/1959; F. 29/11/1965)

Plate 95. **RADSTOCK**. This time looking towards Bristol with the infamous level crossing and the signalbox controlling it, at the end of the platform. Quite a curved station but no check rails. (T. 17/9/1958)

Plate 96. **LAVINGTON**. Looking towards Westbury. Depicts structures typical of the line - brick built station buildings, signalbox and goods shed give a Great Western atmosphere along with rather fine full width canopies. (T. 13/9/1957; P. 18/4/1966; F. 3/4/1967)

Plate 97. **CULMSTOCK** on the Hemyock branch looking towards Hemyock. The cattle pens in the foreground were served by two sidings and the sleepers, yard clutter and platform barrows give a busy atmosphere to this diminutive station - sadly now all gone. (GW1; T. 5/1951; P/F. 9/9/1963)

Plate 98. **CHARLBURY**. Looking towards Moreton-in-Marsh. Whilst a simple waiting shelter suffices on the down platform, upside passengers have the superb Brunelian timber building, erected in 1852/53 for the Oxford, Worcester and Wolverhampton Railway. It is a copy, in timber, of stations built earlier at Aldermaston and Mortimer. The down platform was extended in 1928. The line passing under the bridge (right) is a headshunt for the loading bank. Note the neat flower beds, ex-GWR seats, the array of ground signals and the ornate platform lamps. (GW1; T. 10/5/1963; F. 2/11/1970)

Plate 99. **CHARLBURY**. Showing the rather plain supporting brackets to the canopy but note the fine old lamp. A characteristic water tank is seen at the end of the platform with the large broad gauge style single road, timber-built goods shed beyond. (T. 10/5/1963)

Plate 100. **CHARLBURY**. A fine detailed view of the goods shed, the water tank with its attendant fire devil and a splendid lamp on the cattle dock - the latter was reached via the goods shed line. Note the permanent way trolley on the right and the boards protecting point and signal controls at the barrow crossing. (T. 10/5/1963)

Plate 101. **LYDNEY JUNCTION**. Looking west with a simple waiting shelter on the down platform and the rather undistinguished main building on the up platform - although the latter building does have a pleasant canopy. Clear signs of where the up platform has been extended/rebuilt. Plenty of pigeon baskets, several Great Western seats, a water crane and a signal sited between the tracks all add interest to the scene. Note the two lamps by the level crossing and the signalbox beyond. (T. 1/6/1964; F. 1/8/1967)

Plate 102. **CROWCOMBE**. Looking towards Minehead with the loading dock in the distance by the loading gauge. The robust stone buildings on the up platform are in sharp contrast to the simple wood and brick waiting shelter on the down platform. The 'W' of GWR has been picked out on the ends of the platform seats. (GW1; T. 11/9/1957; P. 4/1/1971*; F. 6/7/1964) * Re-opened by the West Somerset Railway in 1978-9)

Plate 103. **TENBURY WELLS**. Looking towards Bewdley. A fine brick and stone station building of considerable proportions, showing some LNWR influence, contrasts with the simple building on the left hand platform, with signalbox beyond. Note the platform lamps and the cache of platform barrows beyond the white paling fence on the right. The fire buckets are still marked 'GWR FIRE'. (T. 6/7/1961; P. 1/8/1962; F. 6/1/1964)

Plate 104. **PONTRILAS.** With the main stone-built station building and its later extension (nearest the camera) on the left, each having a half canopy. By contrast on the opposite platform we have a small brick built waiting room. Note the old style lamps with their winders, the platform seat with the GWR monogram and the signalbox. Beyond the latter, the double track mainline climbs and curves left towards Hereford, whilst curving off sharply left on a lower level is the branch to Hay on Wye (the Golden Valley Railway) which closed to passenger traffic on 15th December, 1941. (GW1; T. 5/1950; P. 9/6/1958; F. 12/10/1964)

Plate 105. **PONTRILAS** this time looking towards Newport(Mon.) and showing the very short tunnel under the road to Ross, with the footbridge over its mouth - note the steep steps (this footbridge was subsequently removed). The starting signal near the tunnel has a white sighting board . The bay platform on the right was used by the Golden Valley line trains. (T. 4/5/1948)

Plate 106. **COXBANK HALT**. Looking north towards Audlem and Nantwich. On a double track line and having two similar platforms - grit surface with sleeper edges and wooden supports and faces. Accessed by two simple stairways from the adjacent bridge. Vertical planked wooden waiting shelters with a window in the wall facing oncoming traffic and a roof extended to give a small canopy - no doors and only a single lamp - a bleak place on a cold, wet night! (T. 17/10/1962; P. 9/9/1963)

Plate 107. **WHITEHALL HALT**. Looking towards Hemyock, on the branch. Opened in 1933 with its own crossing gates protected by signals. Again a simple wooden shelter, but horizontally planked and with a corrugated roof. A short fenced walkway led to the platform - sleeper edged with wooden supports, with only a nameboard and an old oil drum (for rubbish?) (T. 5/1951; P. 9/9/1963)

Plate 108. **TY GWYN HALT**. Looking north towards Portmadoc with the crossing keeper's house on the right. A neat wooden waiting shelter with windows and a small canopy. Note the substantial fencing and the mesh crossing gates. The platform has a gritted surface and sleeper edging. The crossing was protected by signals operated from a 3-lever frame. (T. 3/10/1963)

Plate 109. **PLAS Y COURT HALT**. The shelter is out of the same mould as those in *plate 106*. Here however the platform is an open planked one on wooden supports, the shelter being on its own supports. A simple wood and wire fence guards the back of the platform and a single lamp once illuminated the halt. A train has just left for Welshpool. (T. 3/8/1961; P. 12/9/1960)

Plate 110. **TYLWCH HALT** looking towards Llanidloes. A downgraded double platform Cambrian station - hence the station master's house and substantial waiting rooms etc - on the line from Builth Wells to Moat Lane Junction. A single lamp remains at the far end of the platform. A very small wooden signalbox on a high brick base once stood just off the end of the platform. (T. 22/9/1959; P. 31/12/1962; F. 1/8/1953)

Plate 111. **CHETNOLE HALT**. Looking towards Yetminster on the line from Yeovil (Pen Mill) to Weymouth. Note the staggered platforms accessed by the road bridge. The platforms are made from old sleepers with the basic shelter mounted on its own supports. Fencing is similar to that in *plate 109*. (T. 10/9/1957)

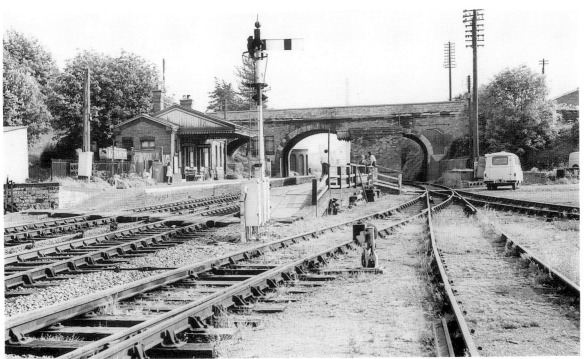

Plate 112. **BLETCHINGTON**. Looking towards Oxford showing how the platforms extended beyond the overbridge. Opened in 1850 as 'Woodstock', it was later known as 'Woodstock Road' and 'Kirtlington'. The up platform building has a small full width canopy looking somewhat unkempt, whereas the smaller building opposite only has a half width canopy because the down platform is quite narrow. Note the loading gauge on the back loop to the goods yard. The spear-head fence on the up platform contrasts with the rather ramshackle wooden one opposite. In the distance the local cement works can just be seen. (GW1; T. 28/5/1964; P. 2/11/1964; F. 21/6/1965)

Plate 113. **BLETCHINGTON**. Showing the direct contrast in buildings with the neat brick built ones on the up platform and a motley mixture on the down platform, looking rather out of place. Beyond the station the lines run over the river Cherwell and the up line signals beyond the bridge have sighting boards provided. (T. 28/5/1964)

Plate 114. **MORETON-IN-MARSH**. A mixed brick building of GWR origin with a slated roof and a variety of chimneys along with a fine canopy. Note the grounded body and the long load leaning against it. The concrete platform lamps are a later replacement but note the curvaceous one attached to the grounded body! (GW1; T.22/5/1953; F. 2/5/1960)

Plate 115. **MORETON-IN-MARSH**. This time viewed in the Oxford direction as a GWR AEC railcar arrives on a service to Worcester. Note the neat flower beds, milk churns by the 'Gents' sign, with the standard fire buckets around the corner. The down platform only has a small wooden waiting room (the left hand side of this platform served the Shipston-on-Stour branch). Beyond the railcar we see the massive single road wooden goods shed with the signalbox opposite. The goods shed and wooden waiting room are O,W & W original designs. (T. 22/5/1953)

Plate 116. **ABERDOVEY**. A Cambrian-built station, looking towards Barmouth, with a fine brick building with full width canopy supported by ornate angle brackets. Note the Cambrian-style platform seats, the barrow and trolley loaded with packs of bottles and the crude water tank beyond. The departing train has left mail for the porter to collect along with the pigeon baskets - beyond them the Cambrian-style signalbox. The down line platform building by contrast is a simple wooden affair with a combined full width canopy. (T. 9/7/1964; F. 4/5/1964)

Plate 117. **ABERDOVEY**. Viewed from the approach road clearly showing the non-GWR style buildings but with a fine platform lamp, some nice spear-headed fencing and camping coaches on the right. An Ariel 'Leader' stands by the platform gate - takes me back to 1961 and the trip I did all around Ireland on mine! (T. 9/7/1964)

Plate 118. **ABERDOVEY**. Looking towards Dovey Junction with a fine array of signals, signs, lamps and a lone Cambrian platform seat. Note the permanent way shed beyond the down platform and the hut, middle distance, where the Aberdovey Harbour branch diverges to the right plunging down a steep incline to the harbour which required 'all brakes' to be pinned down on the wagons. (T. 9/7/1964)

INDEX